THE MANAG... GUIDE TO
UNDERSTANDING
CONFIDENTIALITY
AGREEMENTS

by

Frank Adoranti

Dip Law (BAB), MBA (UNE), FCIS

Solicitor and Barrister of the Supreme Court of
New South Wales

Chartered Secretary

Notary Public

LES50NS

PROFESSIONAL

PUBLISHING

First published in Great Britain. 2006

LES50NS PROFESSIONAL PUBLISHING Limited
A Division of LES50NS (PUBLISHING) Limited
Fitzroy House
11 Chenies Street
London WC1E 7EY, United Kingdom

Email: info@fiftylessons.com

© Frank Adoranti, 2006

ISBN 0-85297-757-3

Cover Designer: Insignia Graphics

Senior Editor: Jessica Perini

Printed by Loupe Solutions

PREFACE

■ ■ ■

Just because you've been signing contracts for years, it doesn't mean you have understood what you've been signing.

One of management's biggest fears is that of an employee exposing the company to the risk of potentially ruinous litigation. It is a fear with genuine foundation.

The cost of litigation is measured in the billions (indeed one estimate is that in the USA alone, the cost is in excess of \$200 billion).

A company exposed to litigation suffers the following consequences:

- uncertainty;
- adverse publicity and loss of reputation; and
- expense and drain of management time.

These consequences are the natural enemies of the manager. They undermine the marketplace's perception of the company and can also have adverse effects on a company's share price. This is especially so given the post–Enron/Arthur Andersen climate of business.

During the last five years, I have devoted much time and effort to instilling a culture of litigation prevention in corporations, by the education of managers in fundamental concepts of commercial contracts.

A common question raised by managers at the conclusion of my seminars is: *What book can I read as a ready reference?* Unfortunately, I found no particular book catering to these aspects of corporate legal education. The most common problems expressed to me regarding existing books on the market were that they were:

- **too difficult to read:** the bulk of titles on the market dealing with contracts are scholarly academic works intended for the practising lawyer or law student;

- **not practical:** the less imposing and shorter "guides" are predominantly aimed at law students "cramming" or revising for examinations or oriented to consumer law issues (neighbourhood disputes, family law, wills and personal bankruptcy); and

- **not portable:** none are presented as handy reference guides specifically tailored to managers. They are usually off-putting in their size, length and/or prohibitive expense.

When discussing the concept of a manager's guide to commercial contracts, most of the comments I received from managers can be summarised in the following quotation:

> *Whilst it might not offer the depth of information on a particular topic that a textbook does, a handy guide in your briefcase accessible <u>when you need it</u> is far better than the volumes sitting on a shelf back at your home or office.*

This provided me with the final impetus to fill the need in this area. You hold in your hands the second in a series of books catering to this requirement.

Confidentiality agreements are almost an everyday thing for many businesses.

To the non-lawyer, confidentiality agreements (like many legal documents) are often shrouded in mystery. The reason being that they often appear as unwieldy documents containing large slabs of text with archaic and confusing legal terminology. They tend to appear intimidating and unintelligible to the non-lawyer, at first glance.

The purpose of this book is to provide an explanation of their function and operation as well as clear demonstrations illustrating their power as well as their shortcomings. The aim is to help companies avoid the aggravation of contract disputes and litigation.

We will commence with a brief foundation of the reasons for using confidentiality agreements and what they can and cannot achieve.

We will then work from a handy checklist of issues in confidentiality agreements. From that checklist, we will dissect a confidentiality agreement and closely examine its various components. From this examination, you will begin to understand the basic building blocks of confidentiality agreements, learn their particular role and how they fit together.

In addition, we will cover a number of practical tips on some of the traps and pitfalls, of which the reader should be aware, when reading confidentiality agreements.

Finally, we will consider the issue of enforcement. How do you make another party adhere to their side of the confidentiality bargain?

The reader will become familiar with the language of confidentiality agreements and will develop a level of confidence to be able to communicate intelligently with-their legal and other advisers. As a consequence, much of the intimidation created by confidentiality agreements, will become a thing of the past.

However, as a safeguard, we recommend that you *always* seek qualified legal advice in specific situations.

When dealing with the law, often, there is no single "right" answer. This series of books will help managers develop the ability to deal with particular aspects of contracts. They should be of assistance to every manager dealing with commercial contracts and agreements. From sales and business development staff through to the CEO and CFO. The series caters to those in large publicly-listed organisations as well as to smaller businesses.

In writing this series, I have drawn on my 16 years of experience in the law in various countries. I have tried to cut through the mire of theory and "legalese" and distil the essence of a highly technical topic into something easily understandable and digestible, for the manager in a hurry.

Where possible, I have used actual clauses, taken from confidentiality agreements I have advised upon, as illustrations of many of the points made in the book.

I trust you find this series of guides as useful to read as I found them enjoyable to write.

FRANK ADORANTI

Sydney, March 2006

ACKNOWLEDGMENTS

A work which is the product of years of research and development never comes together single-handedly. I-wish to especially thank Liz Crowhurst and Lindsay-Powers for their valuable and perceptive review comments on the manuscript and Julieanne Cox for her input into the litigation sections. Their ideas and insights have proven to be of great benefit to the work.

To my editor, Jessica Perini, who continues to endure another book with me, I sincerely thank you for your good cheer and encouragement throughout what has sometimes been an arduous and taxing process.

To my brother Gino for his friendship and support.

To my parents, for their continuing love and devotion; they are my treasures.

Finally, my wife Rosalie — as always — wins my heart by being the centre of my universe and devoted mother to our incredibly beautiful (and always impeccably well-behaved) children.

ABOUT THE AUTHOR

The author has worked in the private practice of law since 1986. Since 1996 he has worked with a number of multi-national corporations both in Europe and in the Asia–Pacific region.

As an international corporate lawyer and consultant, he has reviewed thousands of significant commercial agreements and has seen, first hand, the damage that organisations suffer when proper care is not exercised in negotiating and correctly documenting contract terms. He has also conducted and managed hundreds of millions of dollars of litigation caused by such lack of care.

He has been involved in a broad range of commercial transactions from the sale of a two-and-a-half billion dollar international group of companies to simple confidentiality agreements, and much else in between. He has also assisted organisations with:

● mergers and acquisitions;

● post-merger integrations;

● corporate restructures;

● establishment of tender and bidding processes;

- crisis management planning;

- contract management systems;

- legal audit and legal risk assessments;

- relations with external lawyers;

- planning corporate legal departments;

- compliance programs; and

- in-house training programs and seminars on contracts and other legal issues.

In addition to his qualifications as a lawyer, he has an MBA and is a Fellow of the Institute of Chartered Secretaries and Administrators. He is also a Notary Public.

TABLE OF CONTENTS

▧▧▧

INTRODUCTION

■■■

There are different types of confidentiality agreements that are used for different purposes. This book will cover the most typical form of confidentiality agreement concerning the provision of information from one party to another in furtherance of a contemplated transaction, such as the acquisition of a company or business or the entering into of a joint venture or some other form of cooperative agreement.

The duty of confidentiality in an employment situation is subject to an often-intricate web of employment laws and regulations and is outside the scope of this work.

The aim of this book is to give managers and employees a broad understanding of confidentiality agreements that are presented to them for signature, in the course of business. You will learn the benefits of a confidentiality agreement when used properly and intelligently.

Many managers have little understanding of the nuances of confidentiality agreements. Indeed many have been encountering and reading them for years, often without an appreciation of their full significance.

The current climate of business is one of heightened awareness of risk and of safeguarding proprietary information. An injudicious move with a confidentiality agreement could leave a company's valuable intellectual property unprotected and open for disclosure and use.

In many cases, a company's single most valuable asset will be its intellectual property. Often, such capital is accumulated over the course of many years of continued heavy investment with little or no initial return. It is at the time when such an investment finally produces a tangible or usable result, that such information becomes most sought after. Others may then wish to capitalise on the outcome, without the pain and risk of the investment and initial uncertainty.

It is for this reason that most companies such as pharmaceutical companies, as an example, so jealously guard their proprietary research and other trade secrets.

Directors will have duties in such instances to ensure that adequate processes and systems are in place to ensure sufficient protection of such valuable intellectual property, especially against inadvertent disclosure.

Golden Rule

To protect confidential and proprietary information, *preventative* measures and safeguards are the best tools available. Once the information is already "out there" and available to others, it is too late.

You cannot "unring" the proverbial bell.

Directors certainly do not wish to be exposed to personal liability because they signed a confidentiality agreement that, unintentionally but effectively, gave another party free and unhindered access to private and sensitive information. Worse still would be the case where proprietary rights were actually *given* away.

Depending upon the gravity of such an unfortunate act or omission, litigation could potentially follow from several quarters, almost certainly from shareholders or investors.

Good corporate governance requires that corporations implement proactive programmes and strategies with emphasis on the prevention of unauthorised disclosures in the first place, rather than attempting to deal with them after they have occurred. These factors combine to make a fundamental understanding of confidentiality agreements more relevant than ever.

We will commence by going back to the very basics and explaining what confidentiality agreements are and what they are designed to achieve. Through the use of examples, we will see the differences between fair confidentiality agreements and those that are unduly onerous. Through the explanations provided, you will begin to understand what factors account for these differences and how to spot them.

You will also learn the limits that confidentiality agreements have and why they are not the total protection that some might think.

We will then look at the essential elements necessary to have a complete confidentiality agreement. We will examine each of these elements in detail, so you can begin to see how, together, they form the complete picture.

We will also cover the role of the indemnity in confidentiality agreements.

Along the way, you will learn how unscrupulous players may seek to gain an unfair advantage, at your expense, through the use of confidentiality agreements and how to avoid "getting caught".

Chapter 1

FOUNDATION

■ ■ ■

What is a confidentiality agreement?

A confidentiality agreement is one of the most common forms of agreement encountered in business. You may see it often referred to as a *non-disclosure agreement* or *secrecy agreement*. The terms can be used interchangeably, however, for the sake of convenience, the term *confidentiality agreement* will be used here.

A confidentiality agreement is a binding contract between two (or sometimes more) individuals or entities whereby one party (the Discloser) agrees to provide the other (the Recipient) with certain confidential information, which the Recipient agrees not to disclose or use, other than in the manner and for the limited purpose specified in the confidentiality agreement.

It also serves to provide for the orderly return or destruction of the confidential information supplied in the event that a deal between the parties does not ultimately proceed.

Ideally, the agreement will also set out the obligations of a party to safeguard the confidential information and detail the remedies available in the event of a breach.

In certain circumstances, the exchange of information might be a two-way process with each party having reciprocal rights and obligations of confidentiality in respect of the other party. In such a case the Discloser is also the Recipient of the other party's confidential information and vice versa.

Golden Rule

At its barest essence, a confidentiality agreement must do three things:

1) define what information is confidential;

2) limit the scope for its use; and

3) restrict its disclosure.

Basic terminology

The parties to a confidentiality agreement are usually called the:

- **Discloser** or **Disclosing Party** — the party disclosing or providing the confidential information to the Recipient; and

- **Recipient** or **Receiving Party** — the party receiving or being provided with the confidential information of the Discloser.

The words "Discloser" and "Recipient" appear with the first letter capitalised as they are generally *defined* terms in a confidentiality agreement. Capitalisation in contracts usually means that the reader should refer back to the "definitions" section. This distinguishes words from the appearance of the word when it is used generally.

Commercial agreements will generally have a "definitions" section defining specific terms.

Alternatively, a defined term appears enclosed within parentheses and quotation marks after the first occurrence of the word or phrase to be defined. For example, the definition of a party to an agreement might appear as follows:

Matt Adore of 123 Bull Street, Pamplona
(**"Recipient"**)

or

Matt Adore of 123 Bull Street, Pamplona
(hereinafter referred to as the "Recipient")

Therefore, the continued use of the word "Recipient", after the initial definition, is taken to refer to the full description of the person described in the initial definition.

■ ■ ■

"Plain English" or "legalese"?

As with most forms of legal documents, confidentiality agreements can take the form of either the newer style "plain English" documents or the more traditional "legalese" ones using archaic and unfamiliar (to the non-lawyer) language and expression.

Plain English documents are much more difficult for lawyers to draft. In traditional drafting, one must only consider the legal effect of the words used. Ease of reading is a distinctly secondary consideration. This is why it is common to see long unbroken paragraphs without so much as a comma separating the text. Some sections may have to be read more than once to properly comprehend their full meaning. On the other hand, in plain English drafting (by its very definition), ease of reading also becomes a primary objective. With both considerations in mind, drafting can become an arduous task to ensure that both objectives are achieved.

There are few books on the subject of plain English drafting. One of the leading texts in the area is Michele M Asprey's *Plain Language for Lawyers* (2nd ed, Federation Press, Sydney, 1996).

For the moment, it seems that "legalese" tends to dominate drafting styles, since many lawyers tend to be comfortable and familiar with what they often justify as "tried and tested" phrases in documents.

However, it is useful to bear in mind, as a general point, that the more unnecessary words used in a particular expression, the greater the potential for a misunderstanding or a loophole to be lurking.

To illustrate the point, consider a road-sign that said something along the following lines:

All vehicles including but not limited to trucks (whether articulated or otherwise), motor cars, motorcycles and any other motorised conveyance shall come to a full and complete standstill at the line marked on the intersection prior to proceeding further in whichever direction.

Complicated isn't it? Even though it appears exhaustive and thorough, do you think it would apply to bicycles? The more unnecessary words used, the greater the possibility for errors arising.

Consider the effect of the same sign using simplified and more direct language, leaving little room for error or misinterpretation:

STOP

Chapter 2

WHY USE A CONFIDENTIALITY AGREEMENT?

■ ■ ■

Use of confidentiality agreements

Some firms want you to sign a confidentiality agreement before talking to you about, or showing you, anything. The reason for such an attitude is that most companies have information they regard as valuable and commercially sensitive. For example, they may possess specialised know-how and processes, customer information or lists, research and development, technical advances, financial and other commercial data, lists of employees, business plans, secret manufacturing formulae, etc.

As a result, they need to safeguard such information to ensure that it does not fall into the hands of a competitor or potential competitor, who might then be in a position to exploit such information to the detriment of the company to which it belongs.

Business is all about forming relationships: relationships with customers, suppliers, alliance partners etc. It is at the *beginning* of any such relationship that a confidentiality agreement becomes relevant and necessary.

Parties who do not know one another or who have never previously dealt with one another, need to be certain — to the fullest extent possible — that certain commercially sensitive information that is to be passed to the other will only be used for a limited and specified purpose. This is usually the best method to prevent the improper use of information by the party receiving the information and thereby gaining or exploiting an unfair advantage, through the use of such information.

Checklist: essential elements of a basic confidentiality agreement

QUESTIONS TO CONSIDER AND SPECIFY IN THE AGREEMENT

- What information is to be considered "confidential information"?

- For what specific purpose will the information be supplied?

- Are there to be any exceptions to the definition of "confidential information"?

- Are there to be any permissible disclosures?

POSITIVE STATEMENTS TO BE MADE (IF APPLICABLE, DEPENDING UPON THE CIRCUMSTANCES)

That:

- disclosure is not intended to transfer any rights in such information;

- there is no exclusivity to the Recipient in the confidential information;

- there is no obligation upon the Discloser to provide confidential information;

- the supply of confidential information does not constitute an offer; and

- no warranty is given about the accuracy or completeness of the information.

STATEMENTS OF THE RECIPIENT'S OBLIGATIONS

The Recipient:

- shall use all reasonable measures to keep the information confidential;

- shall be responsible for any unauthorised disclosure;

- indemnifies the Discloser for loss arising from Recipient's breach of the agreement (this is optional and we'll discuss it in more depth a little later);

- acknowledges that breach of the agreement may cause loss to the Discloser;

- shall return all confidential information on demand; and

- agrees not to solicit or approach employees, customers or suppliers.

BOILERPLATE ITEMS (COMMON CONTRACTUAL TERMS)

- Term of the agreement. (How long is the agreement to be in force? When does it start? When does it end?)

- Governing law and jurisdiction. (Under what state or country's law will the agreement be enforced?)

We will now examine the above elements in more detail.

Chapter 3

INITIAL QUESTIONS

■ ■ ■

Definition of "confidential information"

The first clause in a confidentiality agreement is invariably a definition of the type of information that will be governed by the agreement. That is, which particular information will actually constitute the "confidential information".

Sometimes, in order to be clever, some will attempt to define the confidential information as:

All information supplied by the Discloser to the Recipient whether oral, electronic, written or in any other form whatsoever whether or not it is identified as such at the time of disclosure.

Any attempt to do this — of course — should always be resisted. There are two reasons:

1) Not *everything* parties disclose will actually be confidential.

By agreeing to this, you could potentially turn an innocent discussion about the weather, into "confidential information". Obviously, this is an exaggerated example to illustrate the point; it would be rare that a party would sustain damages as a result of the breach of such an "obligation".

One way of dealing with this is by a clause along the following lines:

"Confidential Information" means any information in any form or medium made available to the Recipient by the Discloser and marked "Confidential".

The disadvantage is that if you omit to label something as "confidential", you could "lose" it.

The extensive use of a "Confidential" rubber stamp in such instances might be a wise investment. A more practicable alternative in business will always be the bundling of documents and marking the entire bundle as "Confidential".

Those who may prefer a lengthier and more categorical definition of "confidential information", might wish to add to the above definition (a selection of that which actually applies to them) from the following:

> *including, but not limited to, technical, market, business or financial information, operating results and any information derived therefrom, trade secrets, know-how, methodologies, techniques, principles or processes, manuals, business and marketing plans, market research, strategic plans, forecasts, projections, client, employee, contractor, customer or supplier lists or information, arrangements with other entities, project information, databases, pricing information and strategies, costs and margins, quality control procedures, computer programs, algorithms, integrated circuits, circuit layout or design, source and object codes, test results, formulae, concepts not reduced to written form, technical principles, features or functionality of any product, the appearance, ergonomic features or user interface of any product, product development plans, concepts, designs, plans, drawings, models, prototypes, samples, any invention or discovery, any provisional, pending or completed patent application, any trademark whether pending, registered or otherwise, or any application for registration of any design whether pending, registered or otherwise.*

As exhaustive as the above definition may seem, there will always be something that it might omit. The advantage of the shorter definition above, is that anything becomes confidential information once it is so designated. Therefore, information cannot be potentially excluded as "confidential" simply because its category was missed in the longer list above.

2) Making *all* oral disclosures confidential is difficult and impractical.

Who can remember what was said in a meeting that took place years ago, let alone one week ago? How many managers keep contemporaneous notes of *every* meeting? Further, of those who do so, how many archive such notes in a manner for easy retrieval several years later?

By agreeing to such a provision, you could potentially be exposed to a claim that a piece of information was confidential because it was mentioned to you in a discussion. Potentially, you might then face litigation for breach of the confidentiality agreement.

One solution, pertaining to oral information, is to firstly identify it as confidential at the time of disclosure and to subsequently confirm this in writing within a certain specified number of days thereafter.

If specifically protecting oral disclosures is important, then a clause to the following effect could be useful in protecting the interests of all parties:

"Confidential Information" includes any disclosure that is made orally or otherwise in a manner not in writing provided:

1) *it is expressed to be confidential at the time such disclosure is made; and*

2) *is subsequently reduced to writing by the Discloser and marked 'Confidential' within 30 days of such disclosure being made; and*

3) *a copy of such writing is delivered to the Recipient within such time.*

Obviously, the notion of having to reduce to writing any confidential oral disclosure can become quite onerous upon the Discloser. However, if properly managed, it is one way of disciplining and focusing on what should and what should not be said to the other party in discussions. However, if such a process is not carefully and properly managed, it could prove disastrous to the Discloser with the unintentional "leakage" of confidential information.

> ### *Golden Rule*
>
> As a general principle, courts are reluctant to construe confidentiality agreements — in respect of information that is not, or has ceased to be, confidential — as being enforceable.

For example, applying for a patent for an invention involves a certain amount of disclosure as part of the process. Once that disclosure takes place in the patent application process, contractual rights of confidentiality with a party (in respect of that information) then become jeopardised, if not lost.

It is important that you obtain qualified advice and carefully consider the ramifications of any such process, *before* embarking upon it, to ensure that you are comfortable with the level of disclosure that may be required to the world at large.

Case study: protection of a new and innovative business process — Smartcorp

A hypothetical multinational corporation ("Smartcorp") sought advice about better protecting a particular and innovative business process that it had developed — at great expense — over a number of years.

The results of the development of the process were condensed and incorporated into a highly confidential procedures' manual.

The manual was highly protected on two levels:

1. **Physically**

    (a) by keeping a controlled number of manuals (two) in the entire company and storing them in a locked safe in two separate locations;

    (b) access was restricted to about five key persons within **Smartcorp** worldwide;

    (c) access to the manual was obtained by being signed in and out by two persons;

    (d) photocopying and scanning of any part was prohibited;

    (e) one electronic copy was kept on a CD-ROM stored in a safe; and

    (f) no other electronic copies were kept on hard drives or otherwise distributed.

2. **Legally** — through the use of a carefully worded confidentiality agreement commissioned especially to protect this piece of work. None of the relevant key employees of **Smartcorp** were given access unless and until they executed the specially prepared confidentiality agreement.

Smartcorp so valued this process — and regarded it as the centrepiece of its entire corporate strategy — that it sought advice on ways to better protect its intellectual property by way of patent.

Given that a conventional patent was not applicable to the process, the only option was to consider an *innovation patent*.

However, it soon became clear that the level of disclosure required to obtain an innovation patent, meant that much of the information and the substance of the closely guarded secrets, would become available to the world at large (and particularly to **Smartcorp's** competitors).

Such disclosure would enable others to develop variations on the theme and potentially negate any competitive advantage that **Smartcorp** had created for itself through a massive research and development expense.

The situation outlined above should give you a good indication of why the makers of Coca-Cola have never sought to protect the drink by patent.

They choose to keep its formula top secret and take legendary precautions to physically safeguard the formula. This approach seems to have worked for them for the last 100 years. It also works for Smartcorp, as you have seen in the case study above.

■ ■ ■

Difference between "confidential information" and "proprietary information"

Sometimes, one will encounter the use of the words "proprietary information" in place of the words "confidential information".

Note carefully, that the terms are *not* interchangeable.

"Proprietary information" is a much broader category than "confidential information" and could include information that is not confidential.

For example, this book is the "proprietary information" of the author but it is not "confidential information" (especially considering the detrimental effect it would have on sales).

Even though it is not confidential, it is still protected by copyright laws as the author's "proprietary information".

It is important not to confuse the meanings of two terms.

■ ■ ■

Purpose of information supplied

Typically, confidential information is supplied for a specific purpose in contemplation of another transaction, later in time, between the parties. For example, the Discloser might give a company access to its confidential information to enable the Recipient to evaluate whether it wishes to purchase the Discloser's business or company.

In addition to the obligation of maintaining confidentiality with respect to the information, an extension of this is to limit the use to which such information may be put. That is, it is an additional restriction upon the Recipient further (and specifically) limiting the Recipient's ability to use such information.

It is important to narrow the definition of the purpose as much as possible, to ensure that the information can only be utilised for such a limited and specific purpose.

An example of an *inadequate* definition of the purpose:

> *The Confidential Information is being supplied to the Recipient to enable it to evaluate certain potential business opportunities that may arise in the future.*

This vague wording could almost enable the Recipient to use the information as it pleased, with virtually no limitation.

Golden Rule

A common theme you will find repeated throughout the *Commercial Contracts for Managers Series* is that "**clarity is king**".

The avoidance of uncertainty and ambiguity is one of the best ways to stay out of court.

Using the example shown above, the theme bears repeating and re-emphasising.

A better example of a statement of purpose might be:

> *The Confidential Information may only be used by the Recipient for the sole purpose of evaluating and deciding whether to purchase the Discloser's business, the subject of the Information Memorandum dated X/X/XX being made available to the Recipient on that basis pursuant to this agreement.*

To gain an added measure of certainty, one might add the following words to the statement of purpose:

> *and shall not be used for any other purpose*

An additional provision relating to the purpose for which the information is supplied, could also in some instances — where the information relates to a technological or mechanical apparatus or computer software program — include in this section of the agreement, a category of what is not permitted.

Specifically, this is necessary to overcome the problem of reverse engineering a particular discovery. A typical example of such a clause could read as follows:

The Recipient agrees not to modify, reverse engineer, decompile, create other works from, or disassemble any part or any part of the technical information contained in or extrapolated or extracted from the confidential information.

Exceptions to what constitutes confidential information

As we have seen earlier, not everything disclosed will actually be confidential.

Typical exceptions to the definition of "confidential information" (ie, what is NOT confidential) are usually:

1)   Information already known to the Recipient.

A prudent Discloser might seek a qualification that the Recipient be able to demonstrate such a claim with documentary evidence.

A prudent Discloser may also seek an additional qualification to this exception along the lines that the Recipient is obliged to immediately notify the Discloser of such prior knowledge within, say 30 days, of the date of disclosure, in order to later be able to rely upon this exception.

2) Information already in (or subsequently entering) the public domain.

As a Discloser, it is good practice to qualify this exception with the words:

other than by breach of this agreement by the Recipient.

The "public domain" exception can, in some circumstances, prove to be a problem. Particularly, where information is in the public domain but is not readily available.

An example would be certain information in the public domain that has been gathered throughout the world at great expense over a period of many years and is assembled in a particular way, such as a building services data firm that compiles a list of building and construction tenders. Such a service would be provided upon subscription to architects, builders and building product suppliers.

Obviously, this is a valuable asset and certainly is the product of a significant investment by the Discloser. Simply because such information is in the "public domain" does not mean that it is not confidential.

You could restrict the operation of this exception to something even narrower than "public domain" by using a clause such as:

Information generally known in the trade or business (in the exact same manner and combination as disclosed) in which the Discloser is engaged.

3) **Information acquired by the Recipient from a third party.**

To avoid potential problems, it is generally prudent practice for a Discloser to qualify this exception with the words *by lawful means*.

A further qualification, although rarely used, is the obligation upon the Recipient to immediately notify the Discloser of such receipt from any third party, as and when such receipts occur.

4) **Information that is independently developed by the Recipient.**

This is a variation on the prior knowledge exception. This one can become awkward to police. How would a Discloser easily and conveniently verify a Recipient's assertion of what is said to have taken place behind the Recipient's closed doors? Not very easily. Again, it creates the type of uncertainty that usually requires litigation to resolve. For that reason, it is a situation that is best avoided.

It is usually best to use the documentary evidence qualification in the "prior knowledge" section in 1) above.

As an even greater comfort, a Discloser might also wish to consider adding a further qualifier:

By a person or persons within the Recipient's organisation that has not viewed or had access to the Confidential Information.

5) Permissible Disclosures under the agreement.

Many confidentiality agreements will contain a "Permissible Disclosures" section. This will list the disclosures that the Discloser agrees to in advance.

Typically, such permissible or allowable disclosures might include disclosures as may be required by law, disclosures to lawyers or other advisers and disclosures to nominated individuals (or a defined class or category of individuals).

This aspect is more fully discussed in Chapter 5 under the heading "Permissible Disclosures".

Remember, just because a number of exceptions are expressed to be "typical", it does not mean their use is necessarily *mandatory*. It is important that they be used judiciously and *selectively,* according to the particular circumstances of each case arising.

Consider the situation where you are a potential Recipient and you find one or more of the above exceptions missing from a confidentiality agreement presented to you for execution. If one or more of those exceptions are necessary to protect your company's interests, you should not hesitate to require their inclusion.

Your lawyer is best able to help you with such decisions.

■ ■ ■

Privacy considerations

In some jurisdictions, customer, supplier and some employee or contractor information may be subject to privacy laws governing the treatment of the storage, retrieval and dissemination of such information.

This might include information stored in customer files, personnel or contractor files and marketing databases.

If any of the confidential information to be disclosed falls into such categories, you should ensure (prior to executing a confidentiality agreement) that any proposed actions do not cause you to contravene those privacy laws or regulations.

As the existence and extent of these laws differ in each jurisdiction, you should obtain qualified advice about the particular categories of information that may be governed by such laws, as may be applicable in your jurisdiction.

Chapter 4

POSITIVE STATEMENTS

███

No transfer of rights

As a Discloser, it is good practice to ensure that a statement appears to the following effect:

- reserving all rights in the confidential information to the Discloser exclusively;

- that the disclosure of confidential information does not create a licence or otherwise transfer, either directly or indirectly, any right or property in such information to the Recipient, either expressly or by implication;

- an acknowledgment by the Recipient that all rights to the confidential information and any intellectual property are and remain the exclusive property of the Discloser; and

- the Recipient agrees to execute any document to give effect to this provision.

If you are a Discloser, this is particularly important.

A Discloser should beware of an unscrupulous prospective Recipient modifying the confidentiality agreement submitted by the Discloser. This might occur by the addition of wording, deep within the agreement, which may potentially give rise to such a transfer of rights.

For this reason, you must always carefully evaluate and scrutinise every modification to a confidentiality agreement, even if the party making the changes has explained to you the nature and effect of such changes.

It is always up to *you* to verify that the changes are consistent with what has been described to you.

Sometimes, the explanation of the changes made will not be consistent with the actual effect of such changes. This may not always arise from unscrupulous conduct. It may simply be through inadvertence or a misunderstood explanation from their lawyer that a given set of words meant a certain thing.

If you are in any doubt or if the transaction is significant, you are best advised to consult your lawyer.

It has been known to happen — on the rarest occasions, thankfully — that a Recipient will entirely retype a confidentiality agreement submitted to them so that it looks identical in type font and format to the one submitted by the Discloser. The Recipient executes the document, returns it to the Discloser without comment and asks for a copy executed by the Discloser "for our records".

However, the crucial difference might be something as significant as a transfer of title or licence to the Recipient of the confidential information.

It is up to you to be vigilant to ensure that this does not happen to your company "during your watch".

■■■

No exclusivity to the Recipient

Sometimes, a Discloser may be "shopping" with two, or more, interested parties in the marketplace.

In that case, the Discloser does not wish to have any restrictions placed upon whom it can talk to and with whom it can conduct negotiations.

In addition, the Discloser will not want to be burdened with constraints on what it can and cannot do with its own confidential information.

Therefore, to eliminate any suggestion of the Recipient having exclusivity to the information being implied either in the document or by the conduct of the parties, a prudent Discloser will include a clause such as the following into its confidentiality agreements:

> *The Discloser retains the exclusive ownership and rights in and to the Confidential Information at all times. Nothing in this agreement shall either:*
>
> *(a) prevent the Discloser from providing all or any of the Confidential Information to any other person; or*
>
> *(b) be construed as providing or granting any exclusivity to the Recipient in relation to the provision of all or any of the Confidential Information to it by the Discloser.*

Of course, if you are a Recipient and are being asked to agree to some particularly onerous clauses in a confidentiality agreement, you might counter in your negotiations with the Discloser, by requesting a period of exclusivity with the confidential information.

Requesting a period of exclusivity is relatively common in the sale of businesses or companies, once the transaction progresses beyond the preliminary stages. This is especially so where a prospective purchaser will be investing in an extensive (and expensive) due diligence and requires some degree of certainty that it is not going to be surprised and outmanoeuvred by another prospective purchaser.

■ ■ ■

No obligation to provide confidential information

In the ordinary course, the Discloser should never be under any mandatory obligation to disclose.

The Discloser should always have the final say on whether to disclose or not disclose any information. This is often dealt with by a statement to the effect that the confidentiality agreement does not create or impose any obligation upon the Discloser to provide any or any additional confidential information to the Recipient.

■ ■ ■

Supply does not constitute an offer

A prudent Discloser will also wish to include a statement that the agreement or the act of supplying any confidential information to the Recipient does not constitute an offer of any kind by the Discloser and does not oblige the Discloser to enter into any further or future transaction with the Recipient. Such a statement is set out below:

> *The provision of any Information to the Recipient does not constitute an offer, the basis of any contract, a representation which may be relied upon by the Recipient or any other form of solicitation by the Discloser. The Discloser is not obliged to enter into any discussion, negotiation or agreement with the Recipient or to provide any further or additional information to the Recipient.*

The idea is for the Discloser to not lose *control* of the situation. If the provision of confidential information were — for some reason — to constitute an offer, the Recipient might be able to accept it and then bind the Discloser to a situation it may not necessarily desire.

A prudent Recipient may also request that the clause operate bilaterally, so that receipt of confidential information by it does not constitute an offer on the part of the Recipient to the Discloser.

■ ■ ■

No warranty about the confidential information

The Discloser will usually make no warranty or representation about the accuracy or completeness of the information being supplied. In other words, it is being supplied on an "as is" basis.

There are two ways of dealing with this:

1) Do nothing and accept the clause. The reason being is that confidentiality agreements are, generally, a precursor to a later transaction. If that later transaction does not proceed, the information will not be relied upon by the Recipient, so a warranty will not be necessary.

   In the event that the later transaction proceeds (where the information *will* ultimately be relied upon by the Recipient), that later transaction will be the time to push for and to require the inclusion of the appropriate warranties of accuracy and completeness of the information.

OR, an alternative (and less often used) approach might be:

2) As a prospective Recipient, you might try to qualify the warranty with a statement that:

> *The Discloser warrants that it will not knowingly mislead or knowingly provide misleading, inaccurate or incomplete Confidential Information.*

The above wording however, might not cover a situation where some piece of information has been withheld, which would cause the information provided to give a different or potentially misleading picture to the Recipient.

To cater for such a contingency, the insertion of the following wording may be useful:

> *The Discloser warrants that no information has been knowingly withheld so as to render the Confidential Information provided to the Recipient misleading or inaccurate.*

Notice the above qualifications specifically refer to "knowingly" withholding certain information or "knowingly" providing misleading information.

In negotiations over the terms of a confidentiality agreement, a Discloser hesitant to agree to such a proposition — might in particular instances — arouse suspicion in a potential Recipient.

However, in general commercial practice, a Discloser is not usually called upon to provide such warranties.

■ ■ ■

Warranty from a Discloser

In appropriate circumstances, a prospective Recipient might ask a Discloser for a warranty that:

1) The confidential information to be supplied or the fact of its disclosure to the Recipient will not infringe upon the rights of any third parties (that is, parties other than the Discloser and the Recipient); and

2) Such actions by the Discloser will not give rise to a claim by a third party against the Recipient.

If necessary, the Recipient can require the Discloser's warranties to be backed by an appropriately worded indemnity clause.

Chapter 5

RECIPIENT'S OBLIGATIONS

■■■

Keeping information confidential

A necessary provision is one that the Recipient will use all reasonable measures to keep the information confidential, prevent unauthorised access or disclosure and that it will not disclose the information to any third party.

One must exercise great care, as a prospective Recipient, that obligations to take care of and safeguard information are not *absolute*. Otherwise, they are tantamount to a *guarantee of non-disclosure*. In the realities of business, no organisation is ever able to absolutely guarantee security of information.

Consider the following clause:

The Recipient shall ensure that the confidential information is kept confidential and is not disclosed except as permitted herein.

Notice that the Recipient's obligations in the clause are strict and absolute. In other words, once there is a breach, regardless of how elaborate and extensive the precautions taken, the Recipient is left with no defence for any breach, no matter how insignificant.

By the addition of the three <u>underlined</u> words below, we change that dimension altogether. In the event of a breach, if the Recipient were able to demonstrate that it had taken reasonable steps to safeguard the information, it might then have a sustainable defence available to it.

The Recipient shall <u>take reasonable steps</u> to ensure that the confidential information is kept confidential and is not disclosed except as permitted herein.

In ordinary circumstances, a Recipient should only ever agree to make *reasonable efforts* not to disclose confidential information to others. It is also common (and not unreasonable) to see wording such as this added to the above obligation:

The Recipient shall use the same degree and level of care to prevent the unauthorised use or disclosure of the Confidential Information as it would exercise in protecting its own information of a similar nature.

Case study: hypothetical — maintaining a secret formula

Consider a hypothetical situation involving the owner of a valuable and closely-guarded secret formula — for the purpose of this illustration — it could be something so valuable as the formula for Coca-Cola, Colonel Sanders' recipe of secret herbs and spices or even the chemical composition of Viagra.

Imagine a scenario where the owner of such a secret formula needed to provide the formula for its valuable product to a third party for some kind of evaluation.

Clearly, a simple confidentiality agreement providing for the Recipient to use "reasonable endeavours" to safeguard the confidential information, would not be appropriate.

In such a case (without providing an exhaustive list of *all* the measures that such an important exercise would require), the Recipient of the formula would need to, *at the very least*, agree to the following:

1) To provide a definite assurance and guarantee (backed by a "rock-solid" indemnity provision) that the formula would be protected, under all and any circumstances whatsoever, from disclosure.

2) To prevent any copying of the confidential information by any means.

3) To restrict the number of persons having access to the confidential information to those absolutely with a need to know and name them in the agreement.

4) To have those named individuals personally execute appropriate confidentiality agreements.

5) To implement a strict and well-defined physical security regime that must be followed to the letter to prevent unauthorised access, copying, use or disclosure in any manner.

6) To have an extensive reverse engineering provision (see Chapter 3 for further details).

7) Provisions for the immediate and specified notification steps to the Discloser in the event of any breach, suspected breach or anticipated breach.

8) To comply with the directions of the Discloser in the event of any occurrence of **7)** above.

However, for any guarantee and indemnity to be of any real effect, there would need to be significant substance behind any such guarantee and indemnity.

It is conceivable that any unauthorised disclosure of such valuable formulae, mentioned as hypothetical examples above, would result in enormous loss — sufficient to probably bankrupt all but the largest and most substantial Fortune–500 companies.

The purpose of the case study is to demonstrate that different circumstances will require Recipients to exercise differing levels of care for any confidential information received.

In no case, however, should that level of care fall below the standard that the Recipient uses to safeguard its own confidential information or at least a "reasonable" level of care.

Your lawyer is the person best placed to advise you on this aspect.

■ ■ ■

Recipient responsible for any unauthorised disclosure

A common term is that the Recipient is responsible for any unauthorised disclosure (whether by its employee or agent) and will be liable to pay damages to the Discloser in the event of any such unauthorised disclosure.

This is reasonable, provided it does not extend beyond taking reasonable precautions in safeguarding the confidential information (see **Keeping information confidential**, page 43).

Companies are amorphous entities incapable of actually doing anything with confidential information. It is the people working in and for the company that will deal with the confidential information.

The Discloser does not have a contract with any of the employees or agents of the company and therefore may not have any direct right of action against them. An exception to this is where employees are each required to sign individual confidentiality undertakings with the Discloser (see more in **Permissible disclosures**, page 63).

In addition, the employees and advisors operate under the direct control of the Recipient. Therefore, it is a reasonable proposition for the Discloser's remedy to be against the Recipient in the event of any breach of the confidentiality agreement by an employee or an advisor.

■■■

Indemnity for loss resulting from unauthorised disclosure

Sometimes, a Discloser will require the Recipient to give an indemnity for any loss sustained by the Discloser in the event of any breach of the confidentiality agreement by the Recipient.

An indemnity is a contractual commitment by a party to make good a specified loss suffered by the other party. In other words, it is an acknowledgment and promise by one party to cover the potential liability of another.

Such a clause typically reads as follows:

The Recipient shall indemnify and hold harmless the Discloser against all losses, damages, costs or expenses which the Discloser incurs or may incur as a result of any unauthorised disclosure or use of the Confidential Information.

Notice the clause does not contain restrictions or limits upon:

- the types of losses sustained by the Discloser;

- whether the obligation to indemnify is limited only to direct losses sustained by the Discloser;

- whether the obligation to indemnify extends to include indirect (or consequential) losses or otherwise;

- whether the unauthorised use or disclosure were to arise only through the actions or inactions of the Recipient, or in combination with a third party.

In the event that a Recipient were compelled — by some commercial reason — to accept an indemnity clause, it may wish to make the following modifications to the above clause:

The Recipient shall indemnify and hold harmless the Discloser against all losses, damages, costs or

expenses which the Discloser <u>directly and</u>
<u>reasonably</u> incurs ~~or may incur~~ as a <u>direct</u> result of
any ~~unauthorised disclosure or use of the~~
~~Confidential Information~~ <u>material breach of this</u>
<u>Agreement by the Recipient</u>.

A key feature of an indemnity is that the obligation
created by it can often extend *beyond* that which
would otherwise be imposed on a party under the
general law.

The very concept of an indemnity is to make
the injured party whole again, as if the loss had not
occurred, even if the person who agrees to
indemnify would not otherwise have had any
obligation to do so.

In a confidentiality agreement, the purpose of
an indemnity clause is to **confirm and reinforce
existing liability**. That is, the Discloser will wish
to reinforce the Recipient's obligations by means of
an indemnity.

Typically, in a claim for a breach of confidentiality against a Recipient, a Discloser might not
recover *all* of the loss incurred. The indemnity,
however, will extend to cover losses that might not
otherwise have been covered by a claim for

damages for breach of the agreement. That is to say, in the event of a breach, the Recipient's damages' bill will generally be higher with an indemnity clause than without one.

Some companies (even some of the largest ones) do not routinely forward indemnity clauses to their in-house legal department. Sometimes, the most rigorous scrutiny such a document might receive is by someone who has "seen these types of agreements before". Sometimes, this is insufficient to ensure careful and proper scrutiny to detect anything untoward in the agreement. It is on occasions such as these that the most onerous indemnities and transfer of rights clauses may often "sneak through" undetected.

As a matter of interest, investment banks will generally never accept or sign an indemnity (not even an indemnity for negligence arising out of their engagement to a client). Private equity firms (venture capitalists) will also generally not provide indemnities.

Generally, a prudent Recipient would view the requirement for an indemnity as optional and one that would normally be resisted. On the other hand, a prudent Discloser might wish to seek an indemnity from a Recipient — particularly where the Discloser will be providing confidential information belonging to a *third party*. In such event, a Discloser could become liable to that third party for any breach and loss.

For this reason, as a risk management measure, the Discloser may see the need for an indemnity to ensure that it is held harmless for any such breach by the Recipient.

Golden Rule

It is prudent practice for a Recipient generally NOT to accept an indemnity clause in a confidentiality agreement.

For a more comprehensive discussion on indemnity clauses and a demonstration of specific examples of the use of such clauses, you should consult **Understanding Indemnity Clauses**, the first volume in the *Commercial Contracts for Managers Series*.

■■■

Acknowledgment that breach may cause irreparable harm

Firstly, we shall define some key terminology to facilitate an understanding of the material presented in this section.

Injunction

This is a court order either:

- restraining or preventing someone from committing a particular act, whether existing or threatened.
  For example, a person might seek an injunction to prevent another from chopping down a tree or demolishing a building. These are sometimes called *prohibitory* injunctions as they prohibit someone from doing something;

- enjoining (or compelling) someone to do a particular act. For example, ordering a party to carry out a certain contractual obligation. These are sometimes called *mandatory* injunctions as they compel someone to actually do something.

Injunctions can be *interlocutory* or interim. These are generally urgent in nature and are granted pending a final hearing on whether the injunction should be permanent or final.

Interlocutory injunctions may be granted on an *ex parte* basis. This means that a judge is approached by the party seeking an injunction, in the absence of the other party. The judge hears that party's version of events and makes a decision on whether or not to grant the injunction. The person applying for an injunction on this basis is under a special duty of disclosure to make known to the judge all the relevant facts — including those which may be adverse to its application.

Often, the circumstances requiring a party to seek an injunction can happen after-hours or on a weekend. In such a case, the courts generally have a duty roster for nominated judges to be on call at all hours to deal with such matters as they might arise.

A party seeking interlocutory relief must be prepared to give the court what is called an *undertaking as to damages*. This is the party's binding promise to pay damages to the party against which the interlocutory injunction is granted, if the court later decides (at the final hearing) that the injunction should not have been granted and that the other party has suffered loss as a result. Note that the undertaking is not confined only to *ex parte* applications.

Case study: KHAN – BLEEVIT

The significance of an undertaking as to damages

The *undertaking as to damages* operates to discourage a party seeking an interlocutory injunction from doing so unless it has good grounds and is reasonably certain of its success. This is because the undertaking can potentially give rise to a significant liability.

Consider the example where **KHAN** applies to the court for an interim injunction to restrain **BLEEVIT**, a manufacturer, from releasing a new product onto the market. The reason for **KHAN's** application for an injunction is a dispute over the new product's packaging.

- **KHAN** is successful in obtaining an interim injunction, restraining **BLEEVIT** from launching its new product.

- **KHAN** gives an undertaking as to damages to the court.

- At the final hearing, the court ultimately decides that the injunction should *not* have been granted.

As a consequence, **KHAN** will then become liable (through his undertaking) to compensate **BLEEVIT** for lost profits for the duration of the injunction.

Injunctions can also be *permanent* or final. This is an order made by a court after a formal court hearing, where the court hears both parties' version of events and any legal argument.

The granting of an injunction is at the court's discretion.

Equitable relief

This refers to a court-ordered remedy not consisting of monetary damages.

There are a number of different forms of equitable relief available.

Generally, the most common forms of relief — and certainly the most relevant to confidentiality agreements — are injunctions (also called injunctive relief).

Such relief is granted where an award of monetary damages would not be sufficient on its own to compensate an aggrieved party.

Liquidated damages

This is a concept enabling a party to a contract to place on record (in a contract) a genuine pre-estimate of the amount of damages or loss that it will suffer in the event of a breach by the other party.

If the agreed figure is not a genuine pre-estimate of the loss, it may be construed by a court to be a penalty. Depending upon the jurisdiction, penalties are generally unenforceable since they are said to be contrary to public policy. You should check with your lawyer to establish the correct position for your particular jurisdiction.

Liquidated damages can either be a stated dollar amount or an amount easily ascertainable by reference to a fixed scale of charges or by a simple calculation.

It is designed to overcome the necessity to prove loss in a claim for damages.

■ ■ ■

Now that we have covered some basic terminology, we can return to consider the **acknowledgment that a breach may cause irreparable harm**.

Some confidentiality agreements will contain an acknowledgment by the Recipient that any breach of the agreement *may* cause irreparable harm to the Discloser and that the Recipient will consent to the Discloser seeking injunctive relief. The clause looks something like this:

> *The Recipient acknowledges that damages are not a sufficient remedy for the Discloser for any breach of this Confidentiality Agreement and the Discloser is entitled to specific performance or an injunction or other equitable relief (as appropriate) as a remedy for any breach or threatened breach by the Recipient, in addition to any other remedies available at law or in equity to the Discloser.*

Most jurisdictions will permit an aggrieved party to seek injunctive relief for the breach (or an anticipatory breach) of a confidentiality agreement. However, in order to successfully obtain such injunctive relief, the party seeking it will nevertheless need to demonstrate to the court that it will suffer irreparable harm if the disclosure is permitted, or permitted to continue.

It is acceptable to agree to a clause stating that:

> *In the event of any breach of this Agreement by the Recipient, the Discloser **may** suffer irreparable harm.*

However, you should not agree to wording to the effect that:

> *In the event of any breach of this Agreement by the Recipient, the Discloser* **will** *suffer irreparable harm.*

Remember, that in order to be successful in an application for an injunction, one of the things a Discloser must prove is that an award of damages could not adequately compensate it for the harm it will suffer.

One view on accepting the wording that "the *Discloser* **will** *suffer irreparable harm*" is that it could effectively save the Discloser the trouble of having to prove to a court, that it would indeed suffer such irreparable harm.

Other lawyers would argue that the use of such words in a confidentiality agreement would not be of benefit to a Discloser. The legal rationale being that it is not possible to exclude (by the terms of a contract) a court's discretion and oblige a court to find that the balance of convenience would favour the granting of an injunction against a Recipient.

Assuming the latter position, that a court still required a Discloser to actually prove irreparable damage, the wording could still certainly be used against the Recipient as *evidence of the intention* of the parties.

At the very least, it would be extremely awkward and embarrassing for a Recipient to then have to resile from such an acknowledgment in court.

However, the point should not be lost that to create such a situation of uncertainty is to almost invite litigation. Therefore, it is sensible practice to try and avoid such wording, wherever possible.

Liquidated damages clause

As a Discloser, where you already have a provision such as the irreparable harm acknowledgment described above, you should avoid the temptation to *also* include a liquidated damages clause in a confidentiality agreement.

A liquidated damages provision constitutes a genuine pre-estimate of the damage the Discloser will suffer in the event of a breach by the Recipient.

That being the case, a Discloser will have created an uphill battle for itself in the event that it needs to go to court to seek an injunction.

Equitable relief (such as an injunction) will generally only be available where monetary compensation is not an adequate remedy. The idea of a liquidated damages clause (as a genuine pre-estimate of loss) is clearly at odds with the equitable notion that a Discloser will suffer irreparable damage.

This is an example of a Discloser potentially jeopardising its prospects of obtaining an injunction by trying to be too clever. (See also **Term of the agreement**, in Chapter 6, which provides another example of where being too clever could prove counter-productive.)

Notification in the event of a breach

One further point is relevant here. A Discloser may gain additional comfort with a clause requiring the Recipient to notify it in the event of a breach or suspected breach of the agreement. The rationale is that by doing so at an early stage, the Discloser's loss can be potentially mitigated. The argument is that the result is good for both parties. A typical such provision reads as follows:

The Recipient must:

a) *immediately notify the Discloser of any actual or suspected unauthorised disclosure or use of the Confidential Information; and*

b) *promptly do anything reasonably required by the Discloser to prevent or restrain a breach or suspected breach of this deed or any infringement or suspected infringement of the Discloser's rights arising out of this deed by any person whether by court proceedings or otherwise.*

■ ■ ■

Permissible disclosures

The most frequent exceptions to the non-disclosure of information are those:

- required by law;
- required by advisers such as lawyers, financial advisers and investment bankers;
- required by other specified third parties.

Permissible disclosures required by law

Some disclosures may be required by law, which could include:

1) any notification to a stock exchange upon which the Recipient (or a parent company of the Recipient) may be listed;

2) any statutory or government authority or agency having the power to compel disclosure; and

3) any court of competent jurisdiction (including but not limited to an order of the court, a subpoena or discovery notice issued in any proceedings in such court).

In this situation, a Discloser would consider it wise to also include a provision to the following effect:

> *but only to the extent so ordered, required or requested provided that the Recipient immediately notifies the Discloser in writing prior to any such disclosure being made.*

In response to which, a prudent Recipient, might wish to qualify the above statement with the words such as "where practicable".

For example, if an officer of the Recipient were in a witness box in a court giving evidence, it would not be "practicable" to give written notice to a Discloser when the officer was asked a question giving rise to a disclosure being made to the court.

Otherwise, the officer could be placed in the unenviable position of either risking being in contempt of court if he refused to answer a question or being sued by the Discloser for breach of confidentiality if he did!

It is not uncommon, therefore, to see a clause along the following lines, designed to give all parties the necessary comfort:

If the Recipient is required by law, a court, the listing rules of any stock exchange of which it or a parent company is a member or by any competent authority or tribunal which has the power to legally compel disclosure to disclose all or any part of the Confidential Information or it anticipates or has cause to anticipate that it may be so required, the Recipient shall notify the Discloser as soon as practicable of such actual or anticipated require-ment and shall use its reasonable endeavours to delay and/or withhold such disclosure, where practicable and lawful to do so, until the Recipient has had a reasonable opportunity to oppose such disclosure by lawful means.

Some lawyers hold the view that such an obligation upon the Recipient may not be valid, given that the existence of a legal obligation to disclose could trigger adverse consequences if any attempt is made to delay disclosure. Others consider that the words *where practicable and lawful to do so* are the protection necessary to give the clause validity.

Despite the competing views, the parties may be better off retaining such wording as it would at least operate as a clear and agreed statement of the intention of both parties. It gives the parties the comfort of knowing that:

1) the Recipient must attempt to advise the Discloser; and

2) the Recipient has the protection of only having to do so *where practicable and lawful to do so.*

Specified third parties and attorneys, financial advisers and investment bankers

Specified third parties such as persons within the Recipient organisation with a "need to know" may have access to permissible disclosures as well as external advisers such as lawyers, financial advisers and investment bankers.

Usually, the Recipient in a confidentiality agreement is a company. Remember that companies are amorphous entities incapable of actually doing anything with confidential information; it is the people working in and for the company that will deal with the confidential information.

Recognising this, confidentiality agreements must permit disclosure to certain prescribed or designated persons. Typically, they will seek to restrict the category of persons having access to the information by either providing that:

> *The Recipient will only make disclosure to those persons in its employ or under its direct control with a need to know.*

OR

> *The Recipient will only make disclosure to those persons in its employ or under its direct control on a strict need to know basis.*

The notion of persons *under its direct control* contemplates the use of advisors that are external to the Recipient, such as lawyers, accountants and investment bankers.

Where tighter controls on the use and involvement of personnel (whether internal or external to the Recipient) are desired by the Discloser, the following clause is useful:

> *The Recipient undertakes to take all reasonable steps to maintain a security system which if so required by the Discloser, causes each Representative not already bound by an obligation of confidentiality, before being informed of or given access to any of the Confidential Information, to agree [in writing] to be bound by the terms of this agreement in the same way as the Recipient.*

The word *Representative*, used above, means a Representative of the Recipient to whom the confidential information is disclosed. Often, the words within the square brackets will appear in the clause. This will mean that all persons having access to the confidential information must sign a confidentiality agreement containing the same obligations as the confidentiality agreement between the Discloser and the Recipient.

Depending upon how this is done, this might indeed be desirable from the Discloser's point of view. If done properly (obviously, it will require the above clause to be reworded and expanded), it will then create a direct contractual obligation between the Discloser and the person giving the undertaking. Whilst the Discloser may never sue upon the undertaking, a person might be more compliant under personal threat of litigation by the Discloser.

The notion of using the words *not already bound by an obligation of confidentiality* is useful to avoid one's lawyers or other professionals who are already subject to an obligation of confidentiality, having to go through this process.

Sometimes, in the case of highly sensitive Disclosers (some might call them paranoid!), the agreement might even go so far as to actually annex a schedule of the names of the actual persons who will have access to the confidential information.

■ ■ ■

Return or destruction of confidential information

It is necessary for there to be a statement that all confidential information and any copies or extracts made, will be returned to the Discloser immediately upon demand by the Discloser, or upon a decision being made by the Recipient that it will not proceed with any further transaction with the Discloser, whichever first occurs.

An alternative to the return of such information, is a provision that the Recipient must certify in writing to the Discloser that all copies, summaries and extracts of the confidential information have been destroyed.

Note, however, that in certain circumstances, there may be reason not to agree to return of *all* confidential information. For example certain professional advisors (such as lawyers) may be required to retain records by their governing professional regulations.

In appropriate circumstances, this should be expressed within the agreement as an exception.

■ ■ ■

Non-solicitation of employees, customers or suppliers

Often, confidential information will consist of customer or supplier lists and details of key employees. This is often one of the most sensitive and valuable issues to a Discloser. A Discloser does not want a Recipient to capitalise (to the detriment of the Discloser) upon such information. The difficulty arises where the Discloser and Recipient are engaged in the same trade or area of business and the Recipient is a direct competitor of the Discloser.

The number of customers and suppliers is generally finite, in any given field. Sooner or later, there is a chance that paths will cross, purely coincidentally. In a large company for example, someone might already have plans to initiate contact with a particular customer, unbeknownst to the viewer of the confidential information.

In addition, whilst the Recipient might not directly solicit an employee of the Discloser, what happens if such an employee voluntarily responds to a publicly placed job advertisement?

How does one deal with these conflicting requirements? In the case of employees, the following type of clause — which quite reasonably attempts to balance the conflicting requirements of both parties — may usually be used:

For a period of three (3) years from the date of this agreement the Recipient shall not, and must ensure that the Recipient does not directly or indirectly solicit for employment, entice away or hire any person employed by, or providing services to, the Discloser, provided this shall not prevent the Recipient from employing any such person who contacts the Recipient or a search firm retained by the Recipient on his or her own initiative without any solicitation by the Recipient.

Chapter 6

BOILERPLATE ITEMS

▪▪▪

Governing law and jurisdiction

In the event of any dispute or call for interpretation of the contents of the document, it is necessary to have a statement of the applicable law governing the document.

This is usually accompanied by a statement of the jurisdiction (place) for the settlement of any disputes arising.

Usually, the Discloser (wisely) chooses its own local jurisdiction, regardless of where the disclosure is actually being made.

For example, a Californian company making a disclosure to an Australian company will select

California as the applicable jurisdiction for the adjudication of any disputes arising.

> *This agreement is governed by the laws of California. The parties agree to submit to the [**exclusive** or **non-exclusive**] jurisdiction of the courts of California for the settlement or adjudication of any disputes arising out of this agreement.*

In some jurisdictions, certain information regarding the conduct of some *government agencies* and companies interacting with such agencies, may be subject to legislation such as a *Public Disclosure Act* or *Public Records Act* as exists in some jurisdictions. In such situations, a non-disclosure agreement will be of little effect as it could be set-aside as being illegal or contrary to public policy.

Golden Rule

Take care to ensure that laws such as those discussed above do not compromise the security of your confidential information, in the jurisdiction in which you will be operating. Your lawyer should be able to assist you in this area.

Another form of the jurisdiction clause, may look similar to the following:

> *This Agreement shall be governed by and construed in accordance with the laws of New South Wales, Australia. Each party irrevocably and unconditionally:*
>
> *a) submits to the [exclusive or **non-exclusive**] jurisdiction of the courts of New South Wales; and*
>
> *b) waives any and all claims or objections based on absence of jurisdiction or inconvenient forum.*

■ ■ ■

Jurisdiction — "exclusive" or "non-exclusive"?

The selection of a *non-exclusive jurisdiction* clause could be a "double-edged sword", in that it may allow an opposing party that same flexibility to choose an alternative venue. This may not always be a desirable proposition.

In some instances, a degree of flexibility in choosing an appropriate jurisdiction is not required by the party drawing the contract, such as in the instance of the sale of a company or a business:

1) A vendor is unlikely to need to sue anybody. The vendor's primary concern in the transaction is obtaining payment from the purchaser. If it is not paid, it does not complete the transaction. In such transactions, it invariably tends to be the purchaser who initiates legal action.

2) In the event of the vendor ever needing to initiate litigation, it would generally be in the vendor's home territory. There is usually no reason why it would want to do so anywhere else.

Some lawyers express the view that by making a jurisdiction clause too restrictive (ie, by choosing *exclusive* jurisdiction), they may make it easier for the other party to strike-down such a clause.

Other lawyers are of the view that it makes little difference whether the jurisdiction is *exclusive* or *non-exclusive*. This is because of the degree of difficulty, in practice, of transferring proceedings away from a nominated non-exclusive jurisdiction. English courts would appear willing to do so only in "an extreme situation".

However, given the conflicting views, a more prudent approach would seem to indicate the use of an exclusive jurisdiction clause.

■■■

Term of the agreement

For what period of time will the provisions of the agreement apply? In other words, for what minimum period of time will the Recipient be required to maintain confidentiality?

This will, naturally, depend upon the nature of the industry and particular information being provided. For example, for drug studies, pharmaceutical companies may request anything from five to 10 years. For other information that is less time sensitive, a term of three years might be sufficient.

Depending upon the jurisdiction, one should aim for the shortest period practicable. The reason being that a shorter period may be more difficult to strike down as unconscionable or contrary to public policy.

Some jurisdictions can regard confidentiality agreements in almost the same light as non-compete (restrictive covenant) agreements; where the starting point is that they should be struck down in the absence of any good reason, as being contrary to public policy.

Therefore, caution is needed here. Any attempt to be clever and over-extend from what is necessary could, in fact, jeopardise the very thing you are seeking to protect.

Chapter 7

ENFORCEMENT

■ ■ ■

Litigation arising out of confidentiality agreements is not a common sight in our courts. The reason being that such litigation presents enormous practical difficulties.

■ ■ ■

What a Discloser needs to prove

In order to succeed in any such litigation, a Discloser will need to prove:

- that the information supplied was the Discloser's property;

- that the Discloser supplied information to the Recipient on the basis set out in the agreement;

- that the information was confidential;

- that the Recipient misused (on the basis set out in the agreement) the confidential information;

- that as a result of such misuse, the Discloser suffered a loss; and

- substantiation of the loss actually suffered.

■ ■ ■

Controls on the orderly flow of information

One element in a Discloser proving its case, is proving what confidential information was actually handed over to a Recipient.

As a practical tip, it is important that a register or list be maintained of all confidential information being handed over. Often, in the euphoria of an initial relationship, the parties are so interested in the prospect of working together and the potential for such collaborative accomplishments, that they risk losing sight of the actual documents and material being handed over.

As with any business relationship, this is generally not a problem whilst things are working and people are getting along. However, if the parties (particularly if one of them) decide that they wish to sever the relationship, there will invariably be room for disputes and acrimony over what the Discloser actually handed over and what the Recipient should, consequently, be returning.

Equally, as a prudent risk management measure, a specific number of persons (the fewer, the better) should be designated as the conduits through which confidential information will be provided to a Recipient.

Ideally, one person (close to the organisation's apex) should be co-ordinating the entire process of handing over (and, if applicable, the return) of all confidential information.

When there are larger organisations involved, it is not uncommon for confidential information to be handed over by various people (who may not even know one another) in various departments scattered throughout the organisation. At the time of reckoning, the fact that an organisation has no complete list of what was actually handed over (and to whom), could become a significant problem.

Golden Rules

- Maintain a register or list of *all* confidential information provided to a Recipient including the date, time, nature of the information, its form (document, diskette etc), manner of delivery and to whom it was provided.

- Ensure that the outward flow of confidential information is restricted through as few key people as possible.

■ ■ ■

Available remedies

In most jurisdictions (you should check with your lawyer in your own jurisdiction for certainty), there are three remedies that a court can provide a Discloser for a breach by the Recipient. The court may:

1) grant the Discloser an injunction to restrain or prevent the Recipient's breach of the agreement or its threat to do so. This remedy is often the preferable one to a Discloser because an award for damages on its own will not generally be sufficient to compensate and protect the Discloser;

2) order that the Recipient pay damages to the Discloser; or

3) in exceptional circumstances, grant the Discloser an *Anton Piller order*. The name comes from an English case of the same name where the first of such orders were made.

These orders essentially enable the search and seizure of documents from the Recipient's premises. Such orders tend to be made where there is a risk that evidence required by a Discloser may be destroyed or removed.

Courts will not allow such orders to be used as "fishing expeditions" to ascertain whether such evidence exists.

To obtain such an order, a court will need to be convinced that the destruction or removal of evidence is imminent. Such orders are extremely rare, in practice.

■ ■ ■

Be on the look-out for "tyre kickers"

As with any form of contract, the best form of prevention is avoidance; primarily avoidance in dealing with unscrupulous players. This is where it is important to do your due diligence on the party you intend to trust with your most valuable corporate secrets.

Beware, that in the area of confidentiality agreements, a proportion of the parties involved may not be genuinely interested in forming a relationship with you, with a view to a further transaction at a later time.

In the motor vehicle trade, such persons are called "tyre kickers". Such persons' only interest is in "checking out the goods". That is, essentially, "kicking the tyres" and leaving. Such persons usually accomplish the task by feigning genuine interest and "going through the motions" of someone genuinely interested.

It can be very much the same in business, where some who express an interest in what you have, may only be only "tyre kickers" interested in gathering market intelligence by seeing and knowing about what you have.

■ ■ ■

Potential problems

It is important that you deal with a person or company of substance in such transactions. The world's best drafted confidentiality agreement will not protect you as a Discloser if the Recipient has no means and/or is not located within your jurisdiction.

Entities or persons outside your jurisdiction can create real problems for you when it comes to enforcement of the confidentiality agreement.

Remember that enforcing a confidentiality agreement is not just about a matter of principle. It is all about protecting your valuable and confidential information. In so doing you want to create every advantage possible to help you achieve this.

Golden Rules

- Take all steps necessary to establish genuine interest from the party wishing to have access to your confidential information. Do an appropriate "due diligence" to confirm.

- Don't automatically react to an executed confidentiality agreement arriving in the mail by simply supplying the confidential information, without further enquiry.

- Make sure the other party actually has *something to lose* in the event that they breach your confidentiality agreement.

- Beware of dealing with offshore entities or ones with no substance.

Finding out that enforcement of your confidentiality agreement is going to be difficult or impossible *after* a breach has occurred is highly undesirable and could even amount to negligence on your part. You may even risk personal or professional repercussions, as a result.

Chapter 8

OTHER TRAPS

■ ■ ■

Unscrupulous players

From a legal perspective, confidentiality agreements are relatively straightforward.

However, as always, there are always some contracting parties who seek to gain an advantage through the unfair use of such a document.

You must always be on the lookout for tricks and traps whenever you are presented with a confidentiality agreement that is expressed to be "standard" or "usual".

It is not unheard of for a confidentiality agreement to be drawn in such a way as to transfer the rights in the information disclosed to the other party, after the expiry of a certain period of time.

Golden Rule

There is no such thing as a "standard" form of confidentiality agreement that cannot be changed as circumstances require. As with any agreement, changes are made by negotiation.

Recognise the "standard form" ploy as simply a negotiating tactic.

■ ■ ■

Security deposit

When confronted with a clause such as the following, your suspicions should be aroused:

A Security Deposit of $10,000 (ten thousand dollars) is required to be lodged together with this signed Confidentiality Agreement in order to obtain the Confidential Information.

The Security Deposit will be refunded should you elect to withdraw from the sale process or be rejected as a prospective purchaser subject to not having breached any conditions of this Confidentiality Agreement.

Should the Recipient be the successful purchaser and not have breached any terms of this Confidentiality Agreement, the Security Deposit will be applied against the purchase consideration.

When the time comes for the return of the security deposit to the Recipient, an unscrupulous Discloser may simply allege a breach of the agreement and the Recipient's security deposit is immediately placed in jeopardy or, at least, in limbo.

The Recipient might then have to resort to litigation to attempt to recover the monies deposited only to find that such a proposition becomes highly uneconomic, particularly where the Discloser cross-claims against the Recipient making allegations of a breach by the Recipient of the confidentiality agreement. In such event, a Recipient may end up simply writing the money off and walking away with the experience.

In the event that you encounter such a security deposit clause, there is only one thing to do. Run. In the opposite direction and as quickly as possible, whilst at the same time, checking your hip pocket to make certain that your wallet is still intact ...

Prudent practice would dictate that a security deposit clause should never be accepted and may be a sign of other dangers lurking.

■ ■ ■

Purporting to include directors personally

That same agreement described above contained a further clause which included three references purporting to include the directors of the Recipient, in their respective *personal capacities*, as parties to the agreement.

The intention was to obviously create a situation where those directors would become *personally liable* for any breach by the Recipient:

"Recipient" — if it is a corporation, is deemed to include its directors personally.

The Recipient hereby indemnifies and holds harmless the Discloser against all and any loss and/or damage which the Discloser may sustain or incur as a result, whether directly or indirectly, of any breach by the Recipient of this deed.

These obligations as to confidentiality will remain in full force and effect, notwithstanding any termination of this deed for the period of three years after the date of the termination of this deed and will bind all directors, divisions, subsidiaries, affiliated, related or associated companies, employees, agents and consultants of and to the Recipient.

The tactic, whilst dubious in substance, style and outcome, nevertheless could become problematic and might, at the very least, lead the parties into litigation.

The same advice given in the Security Deposit section applies here. Run for your life! Especially if you are a director.

■ ■ ■

Surreptitious changes to the agreement

This was previously mentioned in Chapter 4 but bears repeating, if only to ensure that you do not fall victim to this sharp and unethical practice.

The situation arises when a Recipient entirely retypes a confidentiality agreement submitted to it so that it looks identical in type font and format to the one submitted by the Discloser.

The Recipient then executes the document (often without question), returns it to the Discloser without comment and simply asks for a copy executed by the Discloser "for our records".

However, the crucial difference might be something as significant as a transfer of title or licence to the Recipient of the confidential information.

You should be aware that there are people capable of such behaviour. Often they will seek to justify their approach by taking the view that any Discloser — especially one that omits actually checking and carefully comparing two versions of an agreement to ensure similarity — is "fair game".

Chapter 9

CONCLUSION

███

We hope you will have gained an appreciation and understanding of the operation of basic confidentiality agreements and the best times and ways to use them.

By now you should also realise the great power that carefully worded confidentiality agreements can wield. You have also seen the potentially devastating effects they can have if not carefully evaluated prior to acceptance.

Confidentiality agreements tend only to be referred to, after they are signed, when an issue emerges and relationships between parties deteriorate to the extent that the "gloves come off". By then, the lines of communication become severely strained or even severed.

Of course, the operation of logic and reason are not at their peak by that stage. Once the lawyers start advising the parties, it is generally in relation to the document, sometimes in isolation of the background and context of the dispute. Each party naturally presents a subjective view of the world to their lawyer. Naturally, lawyers are entitled to accept their clients' instructions as presented (save for any obviously blatant incongruities).

Even if you reach that stage, the knowledge in this book should adequately equip you to understand how the confidentiality agreements can be applied to your particular case. You should also feel more confident in raising and discussing such issues with your lawyer, without feeling completely out of your depth.

You will also have developed an understanding of the basic structure of a generic confidentiality agreement and its various components and how they interact.

You should be able to detect the absence of essential clauses in a confidentiality agreement that may be required to provide you with some basic safeguards. You should also be able to ascertain when another party is being overzealous or overstepping the bounds of reasonableness in their drafting of such a document.

Ideally, you have gained an appreciation of the relevant steps required to critically evaluate a confidentiality agreement prior to accepting it. You will also, be in a better position to gain the most benefit from your lawyer when working with them in your specific situation.

INDEX

Corporate Legal Education & Development (CLED) can assist your organisation

The author of this series, **Frank Adoranti**, is the principal of the specialised legal risk management consultancy *Corporate Legal Education & Development (CLED)*.

CLED is a specialist provider of legal risk management consultancy services to multinational corporations worldwide. Some of the range of services includes:

- legal audits (legal risk health checks);
- devising contract management solutions;
- other legal risk management advice;
- assistance in negotiating major contracts and deals;
- reviewing tenders and advising on major contract bids;
- specialised business consulting activities;
- formulating business and corporate policy;
- devising codes of conduct;
- crisis management planning and events;
- mergers and acquisitions;
- corporate restructuring;
- speaking at corporate functions and conventions;
- conducting training and seminars for management.

CLED provides such services in virtually any country in Asia, Europe or North America.

CLED is also able to assist you in working with the publisher for bulk and/or customised orders of the **Managers Guide Series** of books for your organisation.